Pigeon Racing

Facts and Information
Handling, Health, Keeping, Housing, Breeding, Racing and Training

By: Lolly Brown

Foreword

While this is primarily a book about racing pigeons, the relationship these birds have enjoyed with humans dates into antiquity. Some breeds found their way to Europe with returning Crusaders in the 11th and 12th centuries.

Pigeons carried messages for the Egyptian pharaohs, and images of pigeons have been found in Bronze Age art dating from 2400-1500 BC. European financial markets have changed direction based on information delivered by pigeon post, and men's lives were saved on the battlefields of World Wars I and II by birds later decorated for their valor.

Simply put, no domesticated bird enjoys an older and richer association with man than pigeons. For this reason, it's impossible, at least for me, to write a book about pigeons and not discuss their history, or their fascinating variety.

The pigeons discussed in this text are not the feral pigeons you see perched on buildings and bridges throughout the urban landscape or congregating in city parks. These are birds with impressive pedigrees, bred specifically for their homing ability, flight skills, and physical endurance.

In the rather lengthy chapter on pigeon breeds, I include numerous descriptions of fancy or show pigeons. It is not uncommon for a pigeon enthusiast's focus to alter over time. Someone who begins keeping a loft exclusively for racing may be drawn to the fancy breeds, while another person may tire of the show ring and feel the pull of competitive flights.

Regardless, once these gentle and intelligent birds capture your imagination, you will likely be hooked for life. Controversy certainly exists about the ethics of pigeon racing, and there is no denying that lofts often face greater than 50% losses per racing season.

I leave the material to speak for itself in that regard. Each reader must reach his own conclusions about his desire to compete in the sport and assess his own level of comfort with its risks and challenges. If you fly pigeons, you will lose pigeons. That is, sadly, a fact.

If nothing else, I hope you come away from this text with a greater appreciation for a bird I have often heard described in disparaging terms. People refer to feral pigeons as "rats with wings." As I also know several serious rat enthusiasts, I can assure you both species suffer insult in such a statement.

Even feral pigeons are beautifully adapted to living on the fringes of our modern world and they, like their domestic and well-bred counterparts, are highly intelligent birds.

Consider this. If you were driven 600 miles / 966 km from your home and released in the middle of nowhere with nothing to guide you but your inherent sense of direction, could you find your way home? Without reading street signs, using a map, or programing your coordinates into a GPS? I certainly couldn't, but a pigeon can. That fact alone is deserving of our awe, fascination, and respect.

While the homing instinct is not fully understood, it is so clearly tied to the earth's magnetic field it is now believed that sun spot activity can disrupt a pigeon's ability to navigate. This means the birds are literally attune to the frequency of the planet in a way we humans are not.

This ability has so intrigued mankind that for centuries he has tested and re-tested the pigeon's homing ability – for financial gain, information dispersal, and competition. The result is a thriving pigeon "fancy" far richer and more complex than the non-initiated realize. My hope is to give you a glimpse into that world.

Acknowledgments

I would like to express my gratitude towards my family, friends, and colleagues for their kind co-operation and encouragement which helped me in completion of this book.

I would like to express my special gratitude and thanks to my loving husband for his patience, understanding, and support.

My thanks and appreciations also go to my colleagues and people who have willingly helped me out with their abilities.

Additional thanks to my children, whose love and care for our family pets inspired me to write this book.

Table of Contents

Table of Contents

Table of Contents

Table of Contents

Chapter 1 – Introduction to Pigeons and Racing

A Note on Language: Throughout this text I have tried to write in plain English so that someone completely new to the pigeon fancy can follow this discussion. This is, however, a pastime that is characterized by many unique terms. You will acquire this vocabulary naturally the longer you spend time with pigeon fanciers. See the glossary for examples of some of this vernacular.

Although there are many types of pigeons, especially in the world of "fancy" or show pigeons, in general terms, a pigeon is a bird with a small head, short neck, and stout body. They tend to be covered in heavy plumage and are often confused with doves. Both species belong to the family *Columbidae*, but pigeons are physically larger.

Racing and show pigeons are not the feral birds you see in city parks. A well-bred racing pigeon can attain an average speed of 50 mph / 80 kph over an extended period and fly a distance of 500 miles / 804 km in a day.

Pigeons have amazingly acute vision and are even able to see ultraviolet light. They are known especially, however, for their instinctive ability to return to their lofts from great distances. Generations of selective breeding and training have sharpened this "homing" ability to perfection in those birds classed as "homers" or "racing homers."

How do they do it? They are known to orient themselves by the position of the sun, yet they travel perfectly well at night. They have acute hearing and smell, which may help them to identify their home territory, and the birds are finely attuned to the earth's magnetic field. No one has the definitive answer. It's tempting to say they do it by magic, and for some, there is that element of mystery associated with the best flyers.

One popular method for picking racing pigeons is called the "eye sign." It suggests that ability can be predicted by looking at the contour and shape of the iris and pupils. People who claim to be well schooled in this selection process say the eyes will even tell the fancier if the bird is right for short or long-distance races.

Treating the matter almost like a sort of divination, these fanciers look into a pigeon's eyes with a lens called a loupe, always on a clear day with a bright sky. If they find a pupil that constricts to a fine point, they believe they have a bird that will fly well over great distances.

Others decry this "voodoo" method, looking to more solid

and less amorphous indicators of performance like muscle tone and weight. They consider the aerodynamics of tail positioning, favoring those birds whose tails point down instead of out. Which one is the right formula? Every pigeon fancier racing birds today will give you a different answer.

These birds, in their different forms, are found around the world. The most common wild species in the United States is the Turtle Dove, *Zenaidura macroura*, a small gray-brown creature similar to the now extinct Passenger Pigeon. Other pigeons found in North America include the White Crowned, Band Tailed, Red Tailed, and Ground Dove.

About two-thirds of all extant pigeon species are found in the Australasia region, including the Crowned Pigeons or Gouras that have a wingspan of as much as 13-33 inches / 33-84 cm. While these birds are the largest of the known pigeons, the fruit pigeons are the most colorful. In Europe, common species include the Rock Dove, Wood Pigeon (Ring Dove), Stock Dove, and Turtle Dove.

Not surprisingly, their wide geographical distribution and their great physical variety has brought the pigeon in close contact with man for centuries.

Pigeons in the Ancient World

Although definitive proof does not exist, many records suggest humans raced pigeons as early as 220 AD. In 1200 BC, the Egyptian pharaohs used pigeons to carry messages between cities with information on the flood condition of the Nile River.

At the height of the Roman Empire, pigeons ran a veritable news network, carrying the results of the Olympic Games for organized gambling syndicates. The ancient Arabs so revered carrier pigeons that they were called "The Kings of Angels." In the great empires, only royalty could own the birds.

Unlike horse and riders requiring weeks to deliver information, pigeons kept rulers in touch with the remotest regions of their dominions. Wherever the explorers and conquerors traveled, they found other peoples using the services of the reliable and talented birds. China boasted a well-organized pigeon post, and the birds were also used in India, Greece, and Italy.

Pigeons in Europe

By the 19th century, a pigeon postal service criss-crossed France. In 1815 the Rothschild banking dynasty learned of Napoleon's defeat at Waterloo via pigeon. They sold their British bonds publicly, allowing buyers to believe the French were victorious.

The price of the British bonds plummeted, at which point the family secretly bought up even more bonds than their original holdings at rock bottom prices. The Rothschilds reaped a huge profit when news of the British victory was released — all based on information carried by pigeons.

By 1870, the French pigeon post expanded its service to

London. By the early 1900s, the masses adopted pigeon racing as a pastime, especially in Belgium, and the sport grew rapidly in popularity.

At the same time, Julius Reuter created a news service that still carries his name today, and is, in fact, the world's largest information provider, that began as a pigeon post.

World Wars I and II

The birds also performed vital communication duties in World Wars I and II. During the First Battle of the Marne in 1914, the French advanced 72 pigeon lofts along with their troops while the U.S. Army Signal Corps used 600 pigeons in France alone. The American Navy kept 1,508 pigeons in their service!

One of those birds, Cher Ami, a Blue Check hen, received the French Croix de Guerre with Palm for delivering 12 crucial message at the Battle of Verdun, the last after having been shot. That missive saved the lives of 200 men in the United States 77th Infantry Division.

The use of pigeons in time of war escalated markedly during World War II when the British relied on 250,000 of the birds. Thirty-two pigeons received the Dickin Medal for valor, including G.I. Joe, a bird in the United States Army Pigeon Service.

Pigeon Racing in Belgium

Racing pigeons became extremely popular in Belgium

following World War II, with the number of enthusiasts rising to 200,000 in 1950. The most famous and influential of these breeders and racers were the Janssen Brothers (Fons, Frans, Jef, Vic, Adriaan, Charel, and Louis) from Arendonk, Belgium.

They were the sons of a pigeon fancier, Henri, who began racing pigeons as early as 1886. A man of high principals, he disagreed with the "widowhood" system of racing, using only cocks, which he believed was opposed to the natural order.

When the eldest brother, Fons, returned from World War I, he purchased a red cock, "De Vos van 1919" from the loft of Louis Ceulemans as well as a pigeon from Cas Goosens, "Schalieblauwe van 1932."

Schalieblauwe became one of the most famous of the Janssen pigeons, and the originator of their slate birds. He sired "Rappe" and "Oude Witoger," birds that won a tremendous number of races as did Schalieblauwe's descendants into the present day. All of the Janssen pigeons can be traced to Ceulemans pigeons and Schalieblauwe.

During World War II, the brothers kept their pigeons hidden in the cellars of the Schoolstraat house and managed to hold on to 42 birds. From this stock they rebuilt their loft, although they never kept more than 100 birds at a time. The superb quality of their birds allowed them to maintain total dominance over the sport in their region and to influence the global spread of pigeon racing.

Louis, the last surviving brother, died in April 2013 at age 100. The descendants of the pigeons raised by the brothers can be found in lofts throughout the world and their home at No. 6, Schoolstraat is considered something of a shrine in the world of pigeon fanciers.

Pigeon Racing in the United States

"Homing" pigeons were imported into the United States in the 1860s, with the first club dedicated to organizing pigeon races formed in 1872. In 1880 the Red Star Club of Philadelphia held a pigeon show, which led to the first organized race of "The Atlantic Federation of Homing Pigeon Societies" in 1881.

That group reorganized in 1883 to become The Federation of Homing Pigeon Fanciers of America with the intent of creating a coherent means of recording flights to be entered in a permanent speed record registry.

In 1893 the Federation merged with the League of Homing Clubs to form the National Federation of American Homing Pigeon Fanciers under the leadership of Fred Goldman. Considered to be the father of the sport in America, he was president of the group from 1895-1897 and was instrumental in advancing timing methods for races.

An internal Federation spat led to the creation of a rival organization in 1898, The National Association of American Homing Pigeon Fanciers, although there was little practical difference in the two groups.

In 1911, the formation of the American Racing Pigeon Union was a huge success, outpacing membership in all other organizations dedicated to the sport. It remains the dominant American pigeon organization in the United States today, working to standardize competitions and introduce ongoing technological innovations.

Pigeon Racing in Great Britain

In 1896 the National Homing Union was formed to further pigeon racing in Great Britain. From the beginning, the royal family had a close affinity for the sport, awarding its patronage for what became the Royal National Homing Union and then the Royal Pigeon Racing Association (RPRA). Queen Elizabeth II and the Royal Lofts at Sandringham have been a well-established presence in the sport.

The total membership of the RPRA in 1989 was 60,000 and has been declining since that time. Those fanciers who are dedicated to the sport, however, eagerly anticipate the group's annual show in Blackpool and allow the RPRA to remain a thriving entity.

Chapter 2 – Racing Pigeon Husbandry

Pigeons are lodged in enclosures called lofts. There is no set model for a pigeon loft. Some can accommodate hundreds of birds, others are much more modest. Bear in mind, however, that in designing your loft it will not only serve as a home for your birds, but will also be a place where you will be spending a great deal of your time.

Think about the practicalities. You should be able to stand comfortably in the enclosure and to come and go through the openings without banging your elbows or being forced to contort in odd positions. The birds should be able to go into an enclosed wire aviary or even outside and re-enter the loft on their own. This allows them to exercise, and enhances their sense of connection to the loft as their "place."

At the same time, however, the loft must be constructed in such a way that the birds are protected from the weather, are safe from predators, have perches to call their own, and places to nest. The space must be easy to clean, and simple to secure against predators, pests, and even thieves.

Picking a Spot for Your Loft

In selecting a location for your loft, try to stay away from spots that are too near power lines, trees, or structures with overhangs. Ideally the loft will sit in an area where it can be clearly visible from all directions and is the most attractive landing spot for your birds.

You don't want your pigeons hanging out in a nearby tree at the end of the race instead of entering the loft and having their time recorded as quickly as possible.

Thankfully, you will face few noise-related concerns in regard to the neighbors. Pigeons fly silently and don't make a ruckus in the loft. Neighbors may complain, however, if they don't like seeing your birds, or if they feel the loft is a health hazard. It should be noted though that pigeons do not carry deadly diseases like H1N1 bird flu.

Make sure that there are no building or zoning restrictions that might keep you from building your loft or that might dictate the scale to which the structure must conform. Don't neglect to check with your homeowner association if one is present. HOAs are often the most intractable of all obstacles to adding outbuildings on your property.

You will fare far better with the neighbors if you erect a well-conceived and well-constructed loft that blends in with adjacent structures and is maintained to the highest standards.

Pigeon Equipment

The Internet is an excellent source for new pigeon fanciers to work out their budget in advance of setting up their first loft. Search online for pigeon supply houses and browse through their catalogs to get a sense of the equipment you will need. Some things, like trap doors, you do not want to design on your own, but can purchase and install.

Then there are all the ancillary but essential items like scraping tools, feed and grit hoppers, water fountains – the list can be long and detailed. By doing your research in advance and making friends in the pigeon fancy, you can build your shopping / wish list and attach "real life" prices to all the items.

Any new hobby can become a money pit if you allow yourself to get carried away. Always draw up your budget before you start to build or acquire supplies!

Types of Lofts

Clearly your design must meet your needs, those of your birds, the demand of your climate, and your available budget. Think creatively. If you have limited horizontal space, how can you make use of the vertical? Can you start with a basic loft and allow for future expansion as money permits?

Pre-made pigeon lofts are available from specialty manufacturers and suppliers, but this can be an expensive route. Second-hand lofts are often available through pigeon fanciers clubs, in pigeon magazines, or online on sites like Craig's List or eBay. Depending on the condition of the loft, it may need to be repaired or augmented in some way.

For these reasons, building a loft from scratch or converting an existing structure may be the best option. Minimum specifications include:

- The loft should be at least 8 inches / 20 cm off the ground.
- Allow 3.3 square feet / 0.31 m per bird.
- Have enough room to have one nest box per pair of birds.
- You should be able to stand up straight in the center of the loft.

A first-time loft may be a "work in progress" until the arrangement is perfect for both you and your birds. Always observe the following:

- Do your birds seem content in the space?
- Is there any aggression or fighting in the loft?
- Is the area easy to maintain?
- Are there places the birds are hiding?
- Do you have enough room to move around?
- Can you store and access your supplies easily?

The loft should face east or southeast to get the full benefit of the morning sun, with windows on the east and west sides. Maximizing sunlight makes pigeons happier and more alert.

It is extremely important to avoid overcrowding at all costs. Packing too many birds into the loft escalates aggression, makes the birds restless, and increases the chance of respiratory diseases spreading.

Plan in advance for the number of birds you intend to keep and build accordingly, but also leave room for future expansion.

Do not pick a flat roof design or one that encourage the pigeons to land and sit after coming home from a race. The idea is to get the birds inside as quickly as possible. Force them to land on a landing board attached to the side of the structure.

Flooring

There is some controversy about the best flooring material. Wood is inexpensive and a good insulator, but has a tendency to harbor moisture and is harder to disinfect.

Wire mesh can be used to create a system where droppings fall to a lower level and are easily raked out, but the material is hard on the bird's feet. Additionally, if the droppings are allowed to accumulate they become a breeding ground for fungus and insects.

Mesh does work quite well in attached aviaries where the birds can sun and become familiar with their surroundings. Since the birds are not on the material constantly, the potential damage to their feet is mitigated.

Many loft owners settle on concrete flooring as the best compromise solution. The surface can become very cold in the winter, so plan on some sort of heating system. Make certain that the floor is level, with no areas where moisture can accumulate. For those times when you need to clean more thoroughly, a drain in the floor can be a major advantage.

Some owners use loft bedding on top of a concrete floor. The material can be anything from sand to wood pellets. It is imperative, however, that the loft be clean and dry. Any bedding must be raked daily and replaced regularly. The alternative is to simply leave the floor bare and scrape it daily.

Sectioning Your Loft

At the very least you will need two sections in the loft, one for mature birds and one for youngsters. If, however, you are using the widowhood system for motivation, you will need a way to separate the birds more specifically.

Pigeons are indiscriminate breeders but are monogamous once a mate has been selected. To avoid unplanned pairings, three sections will be needed: one for males, one for females, and one for young birds. A fourth, smaller section, to quarantine new birds until you can determine they are disease free is also highly advisable.

Sectioning can be achieved with simple partitions, but you must be able to move back and forth between them and the areas must be secure. Movable sections of plywood are an economical and easily altered solution.

Nest Boxes

Each pair of pigeons will require one nest box. The birds are territorial and become possessive about their boxes, which is a further incentive for pigeons to return to the loft from a race.

A nest box should be roughly 23.5" x 16" x 16" / 60cm x 40cm x 40cm. If possible, it is ideal for the box to be positioned in front of a trap and to have an external landing section. Line each box with sawdust treated with insect repellent and an anti-fungal agent.

If you are using widowhood as a motivation, you must be able to secure the hen in the box to separate her from the male during a race.

Rather than build your nest boxes, I recommend purchasing boxes from a pigeon supply house. You will be certain you are getting the correct design and all the necessary functional features. Individual boxes sell for $25-$50 / £16.5-£33.

Each box must have a nest bowl where the eggs will be laid. Pottery bowls are easy to maintain. Cleaning the bowl daily is a must so insects will not be attracted to the droppings left by young hatchlings.

The bowls have holes in the bottom to help keep the area dry. Nest bowls sold at pigeon supply houses are inexpensive and disposable, with a dozen selling for less than $20 / £13.

Perches

Perches give young birds their first experience with flight. The same sense of territoriality that pigeons apply to their nest boxes is also given to their favorite perch. That alone can be a motivator for a racer to return to its home loft.

Plan on having more perches than you have birds. Designs vary from "V" perches to box perches. The latter cost more, but are helpful in controlling and catching birds since they can't jump from one perch to the next to get away from you. Also, box perches catch droppings that might otherwise land on other birds at lower levels.

Traps

The trap is a one-way door that lets a pigeon come into the loft, but prevents the bird from exiting. There are many trap designs. It really doesn't matter which you choose, so long as your birds enter the loft quickly when they return from a race. It is imperative that your birds not have any sort of bad experience with the trap, as this will make them reluctant to enter the loft in the future.

Landing Board

The landing board of the loft is positioned in front of the traps. It is the "pad" from which birds enter the loft. The depth should be at least 12 inches / 30.5 cm. Any less will make the birds reluctant to land. The board should also be wide enough to encourage young birds to sit comfortably and become acclimated to their surroundings.

Attached Aviary

The aviary really should not be thought of as an optional addition. Your birds need a place to exercise in the sun and they need a way to see and to become completely familiar with their surroundings. This is an easy and inexpensive addition. An aviary is really nothing more than a wooden framework covered with fine wire attached to the side of the loft covering an entrance hole.

Ventilation

The air in the loft should always be fresh and dust free, never stuffy. The best ventilation allows for the slow movement of air. You do not want to create drafts in the cold months, but neither do you want the loft to heat up in the summer. Wind-powered fans mounted in the walls are an excellent solution.

Since warm air rises, the vents near the roof should be positioned to move warm, stale air out, while those at the bottom of the loft should bring clean, fresh air in. By raising the loft off the ground, you further ensure good circulation, but take care not to create avenues for vermin like rats and mice to come inside.

Cover any openings with plastic or aluminum vents. Be careful not to angle vents in such a way that moisture can get in and accumulate, especially in areas under the loft where mold and mildew can become established.

Ideally the inside temperature of the loft will remain in a range of 50-86 F / 10-30 C with a humidity level of less than 65%. Higher humidity prevents the birds from resting at night. The consistency of the birds' droppings will give you an indication of humidity levels. In low humidity, the droppings are firm and brown; at higher levels the excrements may be watery and green.

(Note that watery droppings are an indication of multiple illnesses. Do not assume that a change in consistency is due to humidity levels alone.)

Closing up the loft at night and during rain storms will help to control humidity levels, but be careful not to cut off air circulation.

Basic Loft Supplies

Don't feed your pigeons on the floor of the loft. The spilled feed will attract rats. Use feed troughs or hoppers made of wood or galvanized steel. Both can be purchased in a range of $10-$40 / £7-£27. Waterers and grit hoppers cost approximately the same amount of money.

Your birds need constant access to clean water. The containers should be refilled and cleaned daily. Never allow slime to accumulate in the water containers. A dirty waterer is a prime breeding ground for harmful bacteria.

Grit is also essential to help the birds digest their food. Commercial grit products contain beneficial minerals, calcium, and salt. There are recipes for homemade grit, but the product is so economical, there is little reason not to purchase it in bulk. Fifty pound bags (23 kg) are available for approximately $15 / £10.

Both grit and feed must be stored in a clean, dry location that is secure against rats and mice.

Loft Maintenance

A clean environment is the best defense against illness in your birds. Droppings must be scraped daily, and the nest boxes sprinkled with anti-fungal and anti-parasite powder. Rake any bedding on the floor daily, and clean the boxes at least twice a week.

Be on the lookout for musty smells or any black marks that indicate the presence of mold. Clean and disinfect water containers weekly.

Ideally your loft should be cleaned at least once a day. This also gives you the opportunity to observe your pigeons closely and to act quickly if you spot any of the warning signs of illness. (See the chapter on health for a full discussion of such potential problems.)

For your own protection, wear a mask while working in your loft and wash your hands with a good-quality anti-bacterial soap before and after handling your birds.

Feed

An average-sized pigeon needs roughly one ounce (28 grams) of food daily. (Birds in training may need more nutrition.) Mothers feeding their young will consume twice as much.

As seedeaters, pigeons have a tendency to pick out what they like and leave the rest. It is imperative that the birds receive a balanced diet that does not include human food like bread. Acceptable feed choices include:

- dried field peas, which are high in protein
- corn, which is an exceptionally good winter food
- wheat
- barley
- buckeye
- rye

- oats
- linseed

Many fanciers prefer pigeon pellets or prepared seed mixes. Both provide solid, well-balanced nutrition. A product like Purina Mills NutriBlend Green Pigeon Feed (50 lbs. / 23 kg for $25 / £17), for instance, contains:

- ground corn
- dehulled soybean meal
- ground wheat
- dehydrated alfalfa meal
- ground oats
- dried beet pulp
- calcium carbonate

The objection some fanciers have to such products is the presence of preservatives. If you prefer to feed your birds only natural seeds, you can certainly do so.

Feed should be stored in sealed containers to keep the material dry and to prevent the growth of mold and bacteria. Introduce any changes in the feeding plan slowly over a two-three week period to avoid gastrointestinal upset.

Offer your birds chopped greens like spinach, lettuce, or cabbage from time to time, especially during the winter months.

Never overfeed your birds. In the morning, handle the pigeons and feel the crop. If there is still food present from the previous night, cut back on the daily food ration. Also pay attention to your birds' attitude. If they don't rush to the sound of the food sack or tin, they're not hungry. Ideally, you should not give your birds more than they can consume in 10 minutes.

Don't feed your birds after 5 p.m. or they will be restless in the night and not sleep. From time to time, hand feed your pigeons to strengthen your bond with them and to make them tamer.

The Food Call

The food call is a necessary part of pigeon training. Get into a good routine with your pigeons. Let them out while you are cleaning the loft and tending to other chores, then call them back in to be fed. A standard method is to shake a can full of pigeon "candy," a mixture of seeds the birds come to see as a treat (especially if they are primarily fed pellets.)

The birds associate the sound of the shaking can with the act of entering the loft, so you can use the same call to get them to come into the loft faster when they return from a race. Always use the same call with your birds so you don't confuse them.

Water

Pigeons drink water to regulate their body temperature and to soften their food for better digestion. In hotter weather, your birds will need to drink more. Always change the water daily, and do not allow the dish to become fouled with droppings.

Grit

Birds do not have teeth, so they eat small stones or sand to help them break down and process their food, which is swallowed whole. The food first passes to a sac in the throat called the crop before passing on the gizzard. Grit must be present at this stage of digestion. Supplying your birds with grit fulfills this vital dietary need and is a perfect opportunity to introduce calcium into their diet.

Breeding Pigeons

Racing pigeons does not require that you also breed birds, but many fanciers choose to do so. Perfecting a bloodline of outstanding flyers is for many an even greater competitive endeavor than entering racing events.

The major goal in breeding pigeons is the removal of any genetic defects or undesirable traits that prevent a bird from performing to its peak potential.

(The following material is intended as an overview and is not a step-by-step guide. As a new pigeon fancier, I recommend seeking the mentorship of a more experienced keeper the first time you attempt to raise young birds.)

Genetic Considerations

A breeding program can affect the flying performance of your loft. If you mate your two best pigeons, both will be out of the "running" for a period of time while they are feeding their offspring. Better to mate an older hen with a younger male even though the results may be more unpredictable.

Regardless of the philosophy you bring to the management of your loft and the breeding of your birds, keep accurate records to track successes and failures and to establish pedigree. You may either inbreed or cross your birds.

- Inbreeding is the system of mating related pigeons in the hope that a trait from the common ancestry will be passed to the offspring.

- Crossing means mating two unrelated pigeons of exceptional quality to achieve the best mix of the traits seen in both birds.

Each bird will have two genes per characteristic, one from the mother and one from the father. These genes will be either dominant or recessive. In the most simplistic explanation possible, dominant genes "win" about 50% of the time, a situation called heterozygous. If however, you have two genes that are identical the offspring will be homozygous. The gene will be passed on whether it is dominant or recessive.

In picking mated pairs, pigeon breeders try to increase the homozygous traits so desirable genetic factors will definitely be passed on. Without accurate records, this is little more than a game of chance. Genetic calculations can become incredibly complex and are well beyond the intended scope of this book, but I think the general idea comes across.

Inbreeding is one method to increase homozygous traits, but it also increases the number of health problems that affect the birds. Excess use of inbreeding means more infertile eggs and more youngsters that die before reaching maturity. Too much crossbreeding, however, means complete inconsistency in the loft. Good breeders strike the correct balance of both.

Newcomers to the pigeon fancy are far better off buying superior stock from a genetically uniform family of birds. At this stage of your participation in the sport, you should be more concerned about training technique and loft management.

By starting with good stock, you can reliably create your own family of birds in your loft for a number of years until you experience a decrease in performance relative to "inbreeding depression." At that stage, a carefully selected pigeon from an outside source should be introduced to the loft to infuse new genetic material into your bloodlines.

Mating and Rearing

Pigeons training for short distance races should be mated in February to be ready to race by April. Birds that will be racing longer distances should be mated at the end of February or the beginning of March.

When the birds are introduced to one another gradually and allowed to become accustomed to each other, they often mate for life. The males strut and coo, puffing themselves up to attract the female's attention and court her. When the birds begin to bill, you can be certain they will mate.

Males may chase females around the loft and attempt to herd them into the nest. This kind of aggression stops when the birds have mated successfully and the first egg has been laid. Often after mating the male pigeon takes a "victory flight" around the loft, which the hen may duplicate.

Both the male and female care for the babies, taking turns resting on the nest and feeding their offspring with crop milk. The parent will insert his or her beak into the baby's mouth and pump the liquid down into the throat. Over time, the babies receive more grit and grain and less milk until weaning is complete. By 6-8 weeks the young birds are ready to leave the nest.

Chapter 3 – Diseases and Health Concerns

Keeping a bird of any kind healthy can be challenging, but racing pigeons are high performance athletes that require solid nutrition and superb husbandry to remain at the top of their "game." Building your flock from healthy birds to start with is greatly to your advantage.

Recognizing a Healthy Bird

Healthy birds have breast and back muscles that are strong and well developed. Their feathering is strong over the entire body. These pigeons literally look prepared to take off in flight.

The skin around the eyes and beaks should be evenly colored and slightly powdery. Look for any gray spots, mucous, or yellow deposits along the jaw and lining of the mouth. It is important to also check for mites or other parasites. A pigeon in top form has alert, intelligent eyes that appear clear and interested at all times.

The bird should pass only well-formed droppings that do not smell. The pellets are firm and are to be greenish brown. Birds with droppings that are wet or slimy or with visible parasitical worms should be immediately removed from the loft. Pay particular attention to the feathers around the anus, which should be clean and dry at all times.

The same should be true of the bird's feet. Pigeons are quite particular about their feet and will only allow them to become soiled when they are ill.

With new birds, practice a quarantine system, treating the arrivals with a ten-day course of precautionary antibiotics as well as an anti-worm agent. Never introduce a new pigeon into the loft until you are certain the animal is healthy.

Do not stress pigeons by over handling. These birds don't like to be constantly "fiddled with" and they certainly don't respond well to loud noises, especially at unpredictable, irregular intervals.

In selecting a healthy bird for purchase, look at the following features:

- The head should be slightly flat on the top and well rounded. Birds with very small heads are rarely as intelligent.

- The beak should look solid and well-positioned with good proportion in relation to the overall build. The upper jaw should always be larger than the lower.

- Pigeons with good conformation are not soft in your hand. Their flesh feels solid and muscular. Pay particular attention to the depth of the chest, which should be large to accommodate the lung capacity needed for long flights at top speed.

- The breastbone should be equally thick and substantial to form a firm foundation for the attachment of the wing muscles. Birds with arched breastbones do not make good competitors.

- Select birds with wings that are not hard to open and that appear supple when stretched. The bigger the feathers the better.

Do not fall for the trap of picking a "pretty" bird. Color is completely irrelevant, but the plumage should have a nice shine, especially at the neck and throat.

When you examine the surface of the wing, it should be flat and "hard." The tail at rest should be the width of a single feather, but not overly long.

Common Diseases

The following are some of the most common diseases seen in racing pigeons. Note that almost all can be completely prevented by excellent loft maintenance. Rather than relying on using medication as a response to illness, I strongly recommend preemptive measure to make sure your birds never get sick in the first place.

Ornithosis

The infectious disease ornithosis affects many bird species globally including pigeons. It is caused by the microorganism *chlamydia psittaci* transmitted via contaminated dust, food, or water. There are two forms:

- Acute, which can be recognized in juvenile pigeons through wheezing, conjunctivitis, and diarrhea.

- Chronic, found in adult birds that exhibit no sign of disease. These are pigeons that have recovered from the infection. They continue to shed the pathogen, which can be passed to other birds and to humans.

A definitive diagnosis of ornithosis can be made from a microscopic examination of a blood smear from a dead bird, or from a fecal test of a live animal.

Other symptoms include:

- blindness in one eye
- swelling of the eyelids

- running eyes
- scratching at the head and beak
- poor conditioning
- nasal secretions
- slime in the throat
- sneezing
- rattling breath and coughing
- unwillingness to fly

Ornithosis is treated with antibiotics like doxycycline and tetracycline.

Trichomoniasis (Canker)

Trichomoniasis is especially dangerous for young pigeons and can cause severe losses. It is caused by *trichomonas gallinae*, present in the throat, beak mucosa, gullet, and crop of almost all pigeons. Adults infect their offspring by feeding them crop milk.

If the pathogen becomes active, there will be a marked decrease in vitality. Adult birds are reluctant to fly and exhibit a reddening of the throat and experience diarrhea. Yellow deposits called cankers appear on the palate and nestlings develop umbilical infections and excrete pungent liquid droppings.

The disease is diagnosed by examining smears under a microscope, although the canker growths are extremely easy to detect. Infected birds should be removed from the flock. The most commonly used drug to treat trichomoniasis is ronidazole.

Paramyxovirus (PMV)

Paramyxovirus is an exceptionally deadly disease. Young birds should be vaccinated against PMV at four weeks of age. The shot is given under the skin on the back of the neck toward the tail, not the beak.

Symptoms of PMV include poor balance, dilation of the pupils, loss of color in the eyes, loss of weight, slimy green droppings, and a twisting of the head and neck.

Coccidiosis

The intestinal disease coccidiosis occurs in pigeon flocks globally and is caused by coccidia protozoa present in the small intestine. Typically the birds ingest a small amount of the pathogen and develop an immunity against infection, basically living in a symbiotic way with the parasites, which do protect them against other intestinal maladies.

If the disease becomes acute in young, unprotected pigeons, it can be fatal. Affected birds show rapid weight loss and excrete slimy green droppings often with blood present. They become lethargic, appear to be puffed up, have no desire to fly, and show increased water consumption. Coccidiosis often appears in dirty, humid lofts.

Commercial coccidiosis treatments are available, but the best protection is to maintain a clean, well-ventilated loft.

Salmonellosis (Paratyphus)

Salmonellosis is the most deadly of the bacterial diseases that can affect pigeons. It is spread through inhaling the pathogen in dust, contaminated food, dirty loft conditions and mating.

Hens can transmit it to their offspring while they are in the egg or through their crop milk. Pigeons that survive an infection are often chronic carriers and pose a risk to the entire flock. There is no foolproof way to identify carriers. The birds may appear completely healthy, but begin to shed the pathogen again when stressed.

Clinical signs of the illness in its acute form include greenish droppings filled with mucous, retarded growth, emaciation, and death. Often embryos that are infected die before they can even hatch.

In the chronic form in adults the joints thicken causing loss of balance, lameness, and torsion of the neck. During molting season, the dropped feathers are often bloody at the root end.

Salmonellosis is treated with antibiotics. The loft should be thoroughly cleaned and disinfected to prevent spread of the disease.

Adeno-coli Syndrome

Adeno-coli Syndrome, also called Young Bird Sickness, is a combination disease in which adenovirus creates a vector for a sudden aggressive attack by e.coli bacteria. An entire loft can be infected with the syndrome in just 48 hours.

Although e.coli is a normal gut flora in pigeons, profuse multiplication of the pathogen leads to severe inflammation of the intestines with bleeding and diarrhea. The e.coli also enters the bloodstream and can invade the vital organs causing systemic septicemia.

In the absence of e.coli, the sick birds can recover in a week. With the added complication of the bacteria, most die in a matter of days. Affected birds show a loss of appetite and lose weight. Their droppings become clear and watery and vomiting is present.

Since no drugs are effective against viral infections, treatment emphasizes preventing secondary bacterial infections, usually with an agent like baytril. Excellent loft management that emphasizes hygiene and minimizes stress is the best defense against Adeno-coli Syndrome.

Hexamitiasis

The intestinal disease hexamitiasis, which causes loose and even bloody feces, is caused by a flagellate, *Hexamia columae*. It occurs most often in the summer and autumn. The pathogen colonizes in the bird's rectum, leading to the excretion of the disease in large numbers. The incubation period is 4-5 days.

Affected pigeons refuse to eat and drink large amounts of water, becoming emaciated and debilitated. Accurate diagnosis is made by microscopic examination of intestinal or cloacal swabs. Many birds remain carriers after recovery.

There is no effective treatment or vaccine. Intervention focuses on controlling secondary infections with oxytetracycline or chlortetracycline.

Mycoplasmosis Catarrh

Mycoplasmosis is caused by a multiple infection with bacteria, viruses, and pathogens of the mycoplasma class present. Since mycoplasma organisms are killed by almost all disinfectants, excellent loft hygiene is the best protection.

Outside the animal's body, the organisms are only viable for a short period, just 20 minutes at a temperature of 122 F / 50 C and 17 days at 68 F / 20 C. Transmission takes place primarily through contaminated water and feed containers, feces, and droplet infection.

Symptoms include discharge of mucus and pus from the nose, wheezing respiration, and inflammation of the throat. The birds will be unwilling to fly and will be awkward when they try. Diagnosis can be made from an examination of a dead bird's air sacs or from a serological blood test.

Like other primarily respiratory illnesses, treatment focuses on minimizing the risk of secondary infections with antibiotics.

Worms and External Parasites

The types of worms seen most often in pigeons are hair, round, and tapeworms. Each of these parasites can cause a bird to lose weight and otherwise suffer from loss of condition.

The affected individuals lose their desire to fly, typically pass watery droppings, and lay infertile eggs. There are a number of anti-worm preparations commercially available including Combi-Worm, Belga-Wormac, Wormmix, and Worm-Ex.

Like all birds, racing pigeons are susceptible to external parasites, including mites, especially after a race. The "passengers" tend to infest the neck, the inside of the wings, and the area around the tail. External parasites are easily eradicated with a product like Harkers Duramitex Plus, which sells for approximately $18 / £12 per 200 ML.

Chapter 4 – How Races Are Conducted

Pigeon racing has been described as a sport with a thousand finish lines, but only one starting gate. Pigeons begin competing at 6 months old and race until they are approximately 3 years old, although there is no rule to this effect. In some cases, exceptional birds may race up to 10 years of age.

Each year, there are two race seasons. Birds that compete in the late summer and fall are born that same year. They are entered in races of 100-300 miles / 160-483 km and occasionally as great as 400 miles / 644 km.

Birds age 1 and above compete in the spring and early summer season in races of 100-600 miles 160-965 km. There are longer races, some in excess of 1,000 miles / 1609 km, but such events are becoming more rare.

Most races are between 50-600+ miles / 31-1000 km. The longest in the United States is 1,118 miles / 1800 km. All participating birds must have a leg band with a permanent identification number that registers them to their owners. Two racing formats are common: club and one-loft.

Club or Traditional Races

Club races are the more traditional way for the birds to compete. Each pigeon keeper maintains the birds in individual lofts. To enter a race, the birds are taken to the organizing clubhouse where officials attach a race ring to their legs and synchronize the timing boxes of all entrants. The rings are either rubber, elastic, or electronic.

The birds are then released simultaneously at a liberation point whose distance from the lofts has been carefully calculated to the nearest yard with a GPS. When a bird arrives at its loft, the race ring is either removed and placed in a sealed timer clock or scanned and recorded on a computer. The distance is divided by the time to arrive at a velocity in yards. The fastest bird wins the race.

One Loft Races

In one-loft racing pigeons owned by different breeders are raised at the same loft from the age of 6 weeks. They are trained together by one person, and released at the same location and time in four races over the course of the season.

This method is believed to be the fairest way to determine

the best pigeons on an equal basis. Electronic timing is used for maximum accuracy. One-loft races have grown tremendously in popularity in recent years and are the events that command the highest prize earnings.

Understanding Timing Methods

Racing pigeons wear an aluminum ring on one leg engraved with a permanent identification number. Traditionally, the leg ring used in races is made of rubber or elastic and carries the bird's assigned number for any given event. The ring is attached the night before the race and removed as soon as the pigeon arrives at the loft.

The fancier takes the ring off the bird and puts it in a metal "thimble," which is then dropped in a timing clock and locked in place. The clocks are small boxes with a crank on top. Each participant's clock is synchronized with the master race clock. When the thimble drops in place, the official time for the bird is recorded. The device is sealed against tampering.

This system is, however, problematic. The bird's time can only be recorded when the band is removed and deposited in the box. Therefore, the official time does not reflect the bird's actual arrival time at the loft. A matter of just a few seconds can easily lose a race.

Also, if a loft keeper has several birds in the race that all arrive within seconds of one another, the rush to get the rings off the pigeons and the time recorded can be uncomfortable and upsetting for the bird. In some cases, the degree of discomfort is enough to discourage the pigeon from returning to the loft at top speed.

Advances in electronic timing eliminate many of these issues. The bands on the pigeons are outfitted with radio frequency identification (RFID) chips. As soon as the bird arrives at the loft, the time is recorded, even if the keeper is not present. A sensor at the loft detects the bird's arrival and automatically sends the time to a computer at the clubhouse.

While smaller clubs cannot afford this type of equipment, RFID timing has become the standard in all major pigeon races and continues to grow in popularity for its accuracy and "hands off" advantage with the birds.

Especially in traditional races the pigeons do not fly the same distance. One bird may complete a 200 mile / 322 km race in 195 miles / 314 km, while another flies 215 miles / 346 km to get home. Times are calculated out to the third decimal point to determine the fastest pigeon's velocity over the distance.

In this sense, it's really accuracy that is the winner in the race, thus the desire to perfect timing methods in line with the best available technology.

Release and Race Hazards

Prior to a race, all birds are transported to the liberation point. For longer events, they are shipped in crates to be released at a distance. When the birds are released, owners are given the exact time of the liberation, the weather conditions on the race route, and an estimation of the birds' arrival time. Then it's a matter of waiting.

Weather is a critical factor in a bird's ability to return to its home loft. It is common for a liberation to be delayed until conditions improve. Although the homing instinct is not completely understood, researchers have determined that at distances of 40 miles / 64 km and under pigeons navigate by sight. Beyond that, the birds apparently use the earth's magnetic field to navigate. It is widely believed that even solar activity can affect a bird's ability to sense direction.

Birds of prey also represent a risk to racing pigeons, but studies suggest that the numbers of birds killed by falcons and sparrow hawks are far fewer than is commonly believed. In 1997-98 the Royal Pigeon Racing Association, the Royal Society for the Protection of Birds, Scottish Raptor

Study Groups, and the UK Raptor Working Group commissioned a joint study with the following results. Of the pigeons lost during the racing season:

- 35% succumbed to exhaustion or simply strayed off course
- 19% collided with buildings, windows, or vehicles
- 15% collided with overhead wires
- 14% were killed by birds of prey
- 8% became tangled in netting, were poisoned, or became mired in oil
- 8% were killed by other mammals including cats

The average loft in the UK at the time housed 73 pigeons. The study indicated that in a typical year, 38 of those birds would be lost to one of the identified hazards.

Chapter 5 – Pigeon Types and Breeds

There are literally hundreds of breeds of pigeons found around the world that fall into distinct categories.

- **King Pigeons** - These birds are raised as food. They are large, pure white birds with pink beaks. Well-meaning individuals sometimes buy King Pigeons to release them, but the breed lacks proper survival and flight skills. In the aviary, however, they make superb pets because they are exceedingly tame and accustomed to humans.

- **Racing and Homing Pigeons** - Most homing pigeons, like their feral cousins, are blue or white, although this is not a hard and fast rule. The birds are raced competitively and kept as pets. Highly intelligent with powerful homing instincts, these muscular and capable birds are real avian athletes.

  Examples of racing pigeons include:

  Ash - An Ash is a light tan Racing Homer without wing bars. Sometimes these birds are called a Barless Mealy.

  Blue Bar - A Blue Bar is a light blue to grayish Racing Homer marked with two black bars on the back part of the wing's top surface. Often referred to simply as a "Blue."

Blue Check - A Blue Check is a light blue to grayish Racing Homer marked with a black checked pattern on the wing's top surface.

Checker - A Checker is a Racing Homer marked with a colored checked pattern on the top surface of its wings.

Mealy - A mealy is a light tan Racing Homer marked with red-brown bars across the back part of wings' top surface.

Pied - A Pied pigeon is a Racing Homer with white feathers on its neck or head.

Red Check - A Red Check is a light red Racing Homer with a dark red to brown checked pattern on the top surface of its wing.

White Flight - A White Flight is a Racing Homer with one or more white primary-flights (the large wing feathers).

- **Feral Pigeons** - Feral Rock Pigeons are those commonly seen roosting on public buildings and accepting food from people in public settings. They may or may not by hybrid crossbreeds from matings with escaped domestic pigeons. The birds have adapted extremely well to urban life, but they should be allowed to live as wild birds.

- **Band-Tailed Pigeons** - These wild birds are native to North America and the Pacific Coast. They have long, gray tails that are banded with a second white band at the nape of the neck. The birds are approximately 14-18 inches in length and have bright yellow beaks and legs. They live in woodlands and at the edge of forests, spending most of their time in the trees.

- **Fancy Pigeons** - Hobbyists and pigeon fanciers keep these specialized breeds and enter them in competitive shows like those held for dogs. There, the birds are judged according to their merits when compared to elaborate breed standards.

As an example of a fancy pigeon breed standard used for how, the following is the standard for the African Owl pigeon. Note that each of the body parts is described for ideal characteristics, with point totals attached:

African Owl Breed Standard

Head (20 pts.): Proportionately large, massive, round in shape; side view circular with eye in center; front view presenting a high crown, circular from eye to eye; full between the eye and beak; cheeks well rounded and full in appearance; wide in gape or "frog mouthed."

Beak, Beak Setting, and Beak Substance (16 pts.): Short and thick, the upper mandible continuing the circular sweep of the head, both side and front view; the upper and lower mandibles of equal substance, meeting and fitting in a straight line which, when continued backward, should pass a little below the center of the eye; blunt at the tip. Color to be genetically compatible with the plumage. Beak wattles: Fine in texture, small in size and covered with a white powdery bloom; should not rise out of the curve of the head, but form part of the curve. Viewed from the front, the wattles should be of a flattened heart-shape.

Eye, Eye Cere (10 pts.): Large and bold; all eye colors acceptable; eye set in center of the side of the head. Eyes showing cracks, splits within the eye or different colored eyes, in pieds only, ie, one bull eye and one colored eye, will lose two points automatically. Eyes must be the same in colored birds. Cere: Fine and neat in texture, circular in shape; color to be genetically compatible with plumage. Ceres that project past the circle of the head must be penalized severely.

Gullet (4 pts.): Wide from side view, thin from the front view, filling in the hollow space at the throat, starting near the tip of the lower mandible and terminating in the frill.

Neck (4 pts.): Rather short, thick at the shoulders and tapering gradually to its smallest diameter under the cheek or jowl; clean cut at the throat, giving prominence to the gullet and cheeks; the back part joining the curve of the back skull in an unbroken graceful curve.

Frill (6 pts.): As ample and well developed as possible, running well down the center of the breast. There must be at least two protruding feathers to avoid disqualification.

Flights and Tail (6 pts.): Short and hard; folding compactly; the flights resting on the tail, with tips nearly meeting; tail carried just clear of the floor.

Legs and Feet (4 pts.): Legs strong and short, but long enough to give grace to the carriage; free from feathers below the hock. Feet rather small and neat. Toes well spread apart. Color bright red.

Size and Shape (10 pts.): Eight inches from front of breast to tip of tail and eight inches from floor to crown. Judges should consider nine inches by nine inches acceptable. Birds larger than this can be considered in class competition, but are not to be considered for special awards. A good small bird should be considered better than a good large one.

Shape: Compact, giving the impression of hardness and vigor; breast short, full, broad and muscular, tapering to wedge shape toward the tip of the tail; back short and slightly rounded from shoulder to shoulder.

Carriage (10 pts.): Bold, alert and upright; the eye in a perpendicular line above the balls of the feet, the breast thrown out prominently, the neck slightly arched.

Color (10 pts.): All colors should be sound, clear and even, including rump, thighs and belly; the hackle luster should be green except in powdered blues and silvers, in which the luster should be frosted in white. Bars of blues should be black; silvers, dark dun or brown; mealies, deep red; cream, brilliant yellow; lavenders have no bars. Checkers should show even and distinct checkering on wings, breast, thighs and rump. Pieds and poor color on all varieties can be marked down, up to five points. Black and blue colored birds must have black toenails. If not, they can be marked down up to two points. In any print pattern the entire body and tail should be of one color shade throughout. Judge should mark down, up to five points.

Representative Pigeon Breeds

Although the bulk of this text is about racing pigeons, fanciers often keep show birds and pets as well as homing pigeons. The wide variety of species makes these birds exceptionally interesting.

Please note that the following is not a comprehensive listing of pigeon breeds, but only a small representative sampling used to illustrate diversity.

See Appendix I for a more complete listing of breeds. It is not in the scope of this text to provide descriptions for all the extant breeds, which is a matter of some debate even among experts. You may also reference *Encyclopedia of Pigeon Breeds* by Wendell M. Levi (2013)

Many of the birds listed in Appendix I are quite rare outside their native countries, to the point that even acquiring an accurate photograph can be problematic.

Aachen Lacquer Shield Owl

A breed of fancy pigeon, the Aachen Lacquer Shield Owl is

the product of years of selective breeding, but may have existed earlier than 1765. Now an exhibition pigeon, the birds were once flyers. The birds are small, weighing around 330 grams / 11.6 ounces, and are all white except for the colored wing shield, which may be black, red, or yellow. They are rarely seen in the United States.

Absy Egyptian Swift

The Absy Egyptian Swift has a long tail and wings and a short beak. This fancy pigeon is bluish gray on the body, darkening toward the tail with the head also capped in dark blue. The neck and upper chest is marked by a white to buff band.

African Owl

The fancy pigeon known as the African Owl is small in size and has a short beak. The birds have a crest of feathers called a jabot, tie, or cravat that runs down the breast. They are somewhat delicate, and must be kept in absolutely dry lofts with no drafts.

Altenburger Trumpeter

The Altenburger Trumpeter is one of many fancy pigeons known collectively as "voice" pigeons. These birds are distinct for their highly vocal cooing, which has been compared to both trumpeting and laughter.

The Altenburger is a beautiful bird with a gray head, iridescent neck in green and purple, pale barred wings over a darker body. Well-proportioned and solid, they have a high forehead, rounded head, and pale eye.

American Bohemian Pouter

The American Bohemian Pouter is a cross of the German Swing and Czechoslovakian Swing. It was developed as a free flying breed and although now a show bird, should still have a strong body and an elongated, upright stance. The birds have typical magpie markings with solid white wings and colored shoulders, globe, breast, back, rump, and tail.

American Giant Homer

The American Giant Homer was developed in the United States in the 1920s and is shown in all colors and patterns. These are large birds that can grow to as much as 2 lbs. / 0.9 kg in weight. Calm by nature, they are not flying birds even though they carry the name "homer." The breed prefers to mill around on the ground and responds well to being herded, which makes them very easy to keep.

American Show Racer

The American Show Racer is a breed dating from the early 1950s. Often called the "Bird of Dignity," the emphasis in this breed is on an upright posture with a powerful head and smooth feathers. This is a highly popular breed at pigeon shows.

Archangel

The Archangel's body is bronze or gold with a highly metallic sheen. The feathers on the wings are black, white, or blue. The legs are unfeathered. In the United States all color forms are accepted, but in the UK only the black and copper birds are referred to as Archangels. The breed is slender of neck and body and is one of the more popular of the fancy pigeons, prized for its beautiful plumage.

Armenian Tumbler

The Armenian Tumbler is bred for color, distinct markings, and flight abilities. The birds may or may not be crested, but all forms have a rounded head. The beak is light pink or black, and the eyes may be pearl, orange, yellow, or bi-colored. The neck and tail may be black or yellow and the legs may be feathered.

Australian Performing Tumbler

The Australian Performing Tumbler pigeon is retained mainly for exhibition. It was developed in Australia and has been a popular flying breed distinguished for its rolling and spinning action. The birds are clean legged with rounded, short bodies. The eyes are pearl in a medium face while the colors present are classics like almond, kite, and recessive red.

Australian Saddleback Tumbler

The Australian Saddleback Tumbler can be both feather

and clean legged. Developed in 1917, the name comes from the markings on the back, which are shaped like a saddle. The birds have either a spot or, more commonly, a stripe on the side of the head. The colors most often seen are silver, blue, red, yellow, almond, black and Andalusian.

Barb

The Barb, also called the English Barb or Shakespeare, is a medium-sized pigeon with a round head and short, curved beak. The short neck extends into a long body. Knobby coral red flesh surrounds the eyes, which are white with black pupils. The birds have frilled "pants" and profuse feathering in white, black, dun, yellow, and red.

Birmingham Roller

The Birmingham Roller was cultivated for its ability to spin and tumble. It can "roll" through a long series of unbroken whirling tumbles looking much like a spinning ball. There is no distance or separate motion between each revolution, and the speed with which the birds contort themselves is almost inconceivable. (Not all rollers perform to their highest capacity.)

Carneau

The Carneau, a short, compact show bird from France and Belgium, is broad at the breast and heavy set. The beak is of medium length, flanked by large eyes surrounded by a flesh-colored cere.

The birds are known for their large size and are seen most often in white, black, dun, yellow, and red.

Carrier

The Carrier, known as the "King of Pigeons," was bred in Persia to carry messages. The birds were consciously cultivated for their superior homing instinct, but in its modern form, this is a fancy pigeon. Enormous wattles surround the beak of this large-bodied bird. The plumage is close fitting, seen in white, black, red, blue, yellow, and dun.

Chinese Nasal Tufted

The Chinese Nasal Tufted, one of the oldest of the Chinese breeds, is a medium-sized bird. It is bred in blue, black, red, and their dilutes.

Chinese Owl

The Chinese Owl pigeon is also called a Whiskered Owl. They are medium-sized birds with a frill of feathers or "pants" at the front of the thighs. The frill on the chest that runs up to the sides of the cheek is called the "whiskers."

The birds have rounded heads and very short beaks that make them poor parents, feeding their young with difficulty. For this reason, surrogate parents often raise chicks.

Cumulet

The medium-sized Cumulet is the ancestor of the Racing Homer. A full-chested pigeon with long wings, short legs, and a well-proportioned body, the breed is of French origin. The birds are white with red flecks on the head and neck.

Donek

In Turkish, the name "Donek" translates as "falling down from the sky." Characterized by unique spiral diving and aerial acrobatics, this is a performance breed.

Dragoon

The Dragoon, a breed used in developing Racing Homers, are a very old breed from Great Britian. They have a short blunt beak on a head shaped like a wedge. They are poised birds, standing stoutly on short legs. Heavily built, with a short neck, this is a substantial pigeon seen in silvers, grizzles, checkers, dark red/purple, and blue.

English Carrier

The English Carrier is a breed developed in Great Britain from the Persian Wattle. It is one of the largest of the flying breeds and originally served man by carrying messages. Today they are show pigeons and quite handsome birds with slender, long, well-developed bodies.

Fantail

An Indian breed, the Fantail (English Fantail or Indian Fantail) is also known as the Broad-Tailed Shaker. The tail stands away from the small body in a fan shape. Both the head and neck are slender, while the stance is upright from the chest. The breed is often used to help train both tipplers and racing pigeons. Common colors are red, blue, black, silver, dun, yellow, saddle, and checker.

Florentine

The Florentine, called the "hen pigeon" for its body shape, originated in Italy. These large birds are seen in red, yellow, blue, black, and black barred with white wings.

Frillback

The ancient Frillback breed originated in Asia Minor. They are handsome and unique birds with ruffled feathers across their backs. They may have smooth or crested heads, and clean or feathered legs.

There are six standard color categories, self (white, black, recessive red, yellow), pattern (recessive red mottle, yellow mottle, rosewing, whiteside), grizzle (silver, blue, yellow, red), shield marked (ash-cream bar, mealy ash-red bar, silver-dun bar, blue-black bar, yellow, red), any rare color (ARC), and any rare color pattern (ARCP).

German Colored Tail Owl

The German Colored Tail Owl originated in East Prussia in the mid-18th century and is sometimes called the Königsberger Farbenköpfe. It is a well-known Russian breed characterized by high carriage and a lordly demeanor. Colors include white, black, yellow, red, and blue.

German Nun

The German Nun or Cross Nun has a colored cap reminiscent of a nun's habit, while the colored tails and primary wing feathers form a cross when the bird is in flight.

Developed in the 17th century, the breed is well known in Russia. These medium-sized birds have a high, tight forelock reaching to the crest on the back and curls on the forelock dropping to the ears. They are seen in light blue, ash grey, silver, yellow, coffee brown, red, and black.

Ice Pigeon

The Ice Pigeon has light blue coloration reminiscent of translucent ice. The birds may be clean legged or muffed. Some have black or white bars while others are barless. The breed originated in Germany.

Iranian Highflier

The Iranian Highflier is bred in Iran for competition in

endurance flying. Although this is a tumbler pigeon, the birds really just flip. The overall flight characteristics are that of a soaring, hovering bird. The wing beats are slower than that of most other flying breeds, enhancing the bird's endurance skills. The breed comes in a variety of colors and patterns.

Jacobin

The Jacobin is a fancy pigeon with a 5-6 inch feather hood surrounding its tiny head. The bird has a habit of keeping its face covered like a Jacobin monk, hence the name. The pigeons, which originated in Cyrpus, are found in silver, blue, black, white, and red. The breed developed from a mutation in the 1500s.

Kelebek

The Kelebek is a Turkish pigeon with an upright stance. It's an excellent flying pigeon with long legs and a wide chest. The wings are always carried above the tail. The birds are known to fly solo and gain altitude quickly when given a start, which they can maintain for long periods of time. Colors vary by region, but are generally pied or self.

Kiev Tumbler

The Kiev Tumbler is a flying breed of medium height with a long face and long break. A little smaller than most homing pigeons, these slender, gentle birds weigh 210-250 grams / 7.4 – 8.8 ounces. They have small, muffed legs, a crested peak, and carry their wings over their tail. Colors include red, yellow, black, and blue bar.

King

The King pigeon is a cross of the Dragoon, Duchess, Florentine, and Swiss Mondaine. A medium-sized bird weighing around 35 ounces / 963 grams, this American bred original has bright red legs and cere. The well-rounded head crowns a chunky body seen in silver, white, blue, dun, red, and yellow.

Komorner Tumbler

The Komorner Tumbler has both an American and European variety typically treated as individual breeds. Komorners originated in the Austrian Empire in the 18th century and were bred for acrobatic flying. In modern times, however, these birds are rarely free flown.

They are slim and small with a crest that runs from ear to ear with terminal rosettes. Most birds have a magpie pattern in colors of black, blue, red, silver, yellow, or dun.

Lahore

The Lahore is a Pakistani breed imported into Germany in the late 19th century that became popular in the 1960s. Once a meat pigeon, these large birds are now raised for their beautiful patterns and colorful plumage.

Secondary colors at the juncture of the beak and wattle arc over the eyes, with more color over the back and wings.

The body is white, as are the rump and tail.

The birds have broad, full chests that are heavily feathered. Color include brown, black, red, blue, blue bar, and checkered.

Magpie

The Magpie is a graceful, small pigeon with a streamlined body profile. The snake-like neck ends in a small head. The body, wings, shoulder, and legs are all white, while the head, neck, chest, rump, and back tail are colored. Shades include black, blue, silver, cream, yellow, red, and dun.

Maltese

The Maltese is a large, hen-shaped pigeon now bred for show. It has long, straight legs, straight tail feathers, and a straight neck with an upright stance. The breed originated in Germany and Austria. Accepted colors include, dun, yellow, red, blue, silver, and black.

Modena

The Modena is an Italian breed developed in the city of Modena as aerial sporting birds trained to fly by flag signals. They have short, cobby bodies and comes in more than 100 varieties.

Old German Owl

The Old German Owl is the forerunner of the German

Shield Owls. The birds resemble the silver gull with their round, broad heads and arched foreheads. The small but full shell crest closes with rosettes. The body color is white, with wings of blue, recessive red, ash red, brown, and checks. The bars are red, brown, black, white, and dilutes.

Oriental Frill

The Oriental Frill is a beautiful pigeon with a frill of feathers at the breast. Peaked crests rise to the highest point of the head accentuating the shortness of the beak. Developed in Turkey, there are several varieties including Turbiteens, Oriental Turbits, Blondinettes, and Satinettes.

Scandaroon

In its shape, size, and bearing the Scandaroon resembles the Carrier pigeon. The beak, however, is longer and more curved. The breed originated in Baghdad and is found in black, white, red, blue, and yellow. The markings are similar to that of a magpie.

Schmalkender Moorhead (Mohrenkopf)

The Schmalkender Moorhead (Mohrenkopf) pigeon was, at one time, called the Mane pigeon. Monks in the monastery developed the breed in the German town of Schmalkalden. The birds were popular before World War II, but were almost wiped out completely during the fighting.

The breed is docile and easily kept, coming in blue, silver, red, yellow, dun, and lavender. They are primarily white pigeons, with black capped heads and black tail feathers. The feet are extravagantly feathered and the neck feathers ruffle upward.

Schoneberger Streifige Tumbler

The Schoneberger Streifige Tumbler was developed from the Berlin Streiflge and white, short-faced Racing Homers. They are short, clean-legged birds, with a low-slung, side stance. Their heads are small, with high foreheads that are both wide and rounded. The plumage is white with red or yellow bars on a ground color of bluish white (for red stripe) and creamy white (for yellow stripes).

Seraphim Pigeon

The Seraphim Pigeon is an all-white, long-faced, slim pigeon that looks very like a dove. Genetically they are yellow and red, but as adults turn pure white after their first molt. Seraphims hold their heads high, chest pushed forward, and tail held low. They have a pronounced frill, and clearly delineated wings. Each toe is covered in white feathers giving the foot the appearance of a star.

Serbian Highflier

The Serbian Highflier is a pigeon bred for endurance. The birds can make long, circling flights of as much as 15 hours, flying as high as 1,500 meters / 4,921 ft. They were developed in the city of Belgrade in Yugoslavia. There is a crest of upturned feathers behind the head which is spade shaped. The breed is rarely found outside its country of origin, where it competes in performance flying contests.

Shack Kee

The Shack Kee pigeon is a utility (food) breed developed for size and fast production in the Kwong Tung province of China in the town of Shack Kee. They are large pigeons, weighing 24-34 ounces / 680 – 963 grams. The birds are, for the most part, clean legged and plain headed. Though no attention is paid to color, the birds are found in red, red barred, black, blue checkered, blue barred, brown checkered, brown barred, grizzled, splashed, and white.

Shakhsharli

Shakhsharlis are strikingly beautiful birds that make superb racing homers. The birds bond well with their caretakers and are pleasant to keep. The Shakhsharli is a small bird, weighing 12-15 ounces (340-425 grams.) They are broad at the breast with a good wing span and a proud, bold stance.

The feet are muffed, with the feathers reaching to the end of the toe nails. The original colors are blue, red, black, and yellow, but they are also found in ash red, bronze, dun, blue, silver, cream bar, sulfur, and red bar.

Show Cumulet

The Show Cumulet was developed in Germany and was used in Belgium to produce the Racing Homer. The birds have long heads with an even sweep. The bodies are medium and symmetrical with full chests and strong sing butts. The overall carriage is graceful and lively. Accepted colors are white self, or marked with fawny red at the hackle of the neck. The legs are red and the eyes are pure opal with white pupils.

South German Monk

The South German Monk is either clean legged and peak crested or has medium muffs blending into the hock feathers and a shell crest. The bird is white with colored wing coverts.

Strasser

The Strasser was originally a utility pigeon from Austria that has become a popular fancy breed. The birds have a colored head, with color on the head and neck as well as the wings, tail, and back. The remainder of the bird is all white. Acceptable colors include blue, blue barred, black, white barred, black lace, blue checkered, red, yellow, and lark colors.

Tippler

A Tipper pigeon is a flying machine with the capability of staying airborne for as much as 24 hours. The official record in competition is 22 hours 5 minutes. The birds have exceptionally long, broad primary feathers that allow them to fly with incredible ease. All aspects of their build and plumage is designed for maximum aerodynamics, including their clean legs and plain heads.

Turbit

The Turbit is a beautiful pigeon with a white body and wing feathers in yellow, red, blue, black, or dun. The breed originated in England, France, or Germany. They are hardy birds and easy to tend.

Ural Striped Maned Pigeon

The Ural Striped Maned Pigeon was developed in the 18th century. The birds are small and white, with manes that form ovals, crescents, or triangles. The red tail sports a 2-3 cm / 0.8 – 1.1 inches white stripe with a white or red on the underside.

Zitterhall (Stargarder Zitterhals, Stargard Shaker)

Zitterhalls, developed in Pomerania in the 1700s, are characterized by their long, curving swan-like necks. The breed, like fantail pigeons, tremble or shake. They are long, slender birds with an upright posture.

The back is hollow and not overly broad, while the medium breast sits pushed far forward. The birds are clean legged with close fitting feathers in white, black, red, yellow, and blue barred.

Chapter 6 – The Basics of Training Your Pigeons

Young pigeons are initially housed in separate lofts until they reach 5 weeks of age, at which time they are moved to the main racing loft. Most young birds need approximately 6 months of training before competing for the first time.

The racing loft is not only the bird's home; it is also the finish line of the race. Birds must be taught to enter the loft at the owner's signal, usually a whistle and shaking a feed can. Some fanciers also call their birds with a verbal cue. The important thing is to be absolutely consistent.

Birds must be taught to love their home and their keepers. Until they have this sense of home, they are not allowed to fly at a great distance or they may not return. Clearly when birds are released they are free to go where they please. The instinct is called "homing" for a reason.

They are returning to the place they love and the things they love – their keeper, their mate, their offspring, even their favorite perch in the loft.

Training Tosses

A racing pigeon is only as good as his ability to find its way home. The strength of that instinct is often more important than speed. Training tosses are designed to take birds away from home at progressively greater distances to build both their confidence and their physical conditioning.

One of the most common motivational techniques used in the sport is called widowhood. A pigeon is allowed to mate and sire offspring before being separated from his family. Each time he successfully returns from a flight, he is allowed to spend time with his "wife and children," which strengthens the homing drive.

Trainers work with more than one bird at a time, generally in pairs. This allows the birds to be weaned, vaccinated, and routed at the same time. Routing or ranging is the process of allowing young birds to come and go as they please for 1-1.5 hours at a time.

Ranging allows the birds to get some exercise, become familiar with the area around their home loft, and begin to develop their homing instinct. The first actual training "toss" or release is generally at a distance of about 2-3 miles / 3-5 km from the loft. The birds should be released early in the morning (around 7 a.m.) on a clear, still day.

After about 2 weeks, the distance can be increased. A good initial milestone that indicates positive progress is when your birds can return to the loft from a distance of 20 miles / 32 km in about 2 hours. At that point, you are seriously training your birds as competitors.

Intersperse release days with rest days and progressively increase the distances until you are within the parameters of the race in which your birds will compete. As your birds become stronger and more adept at homing, they will need to be trained only twice per week.

Having said all this, understand that every pigeon fancier has his own methods and ideas about training schedules. The best method is the one that works for you and your birds and that delivers the optimal results.

Food Management and Training

For the first four weeks of a squab's life, the birds receive high protein food from their parents through crop milk. By week five, the young pigeons should start learning to take food on their own, a process that can take up to two weeks. It is after weaning that a pigeon begins to learn to perch.

(It is important to place the birds in separate compartments after weaning to avoid unplanned mating.)

Dietary protein is reduced after weaning to lessen the chance of weight gain and to prevent excessive molting. This can be accomplished by ensuring that barley accounts for about a third of the pigeon's overall consumption. Less protein intake keeps the birds agile and more responsive to training.

When pigeons return to the loft, they should always find food and water on the other side of the trapping flap. Make sure that the birds in the loft have already eaten so the racers get all of the available food.

Racing pigeons are essentially marathon runners. Young birds in particular fly at top speed and do not conserve their energy. Having food ready for them is a nutritional necessity for physical recovery. You may even choose to mix vitamin supplements in the food and water to replenish glucose and electrolyte levels.

The post-race feeding also reinforces the bird's homing instinct. Knowing that a good meal is waiting at the loft encourages them to go inside immediately. This gives you the opportunity to remove their elastic race band and to record their arrival as quickly as possible.

(Many fanciers who do not like the widowhood method of building motivation concentrate more on this kind of positive reinforcement, reasoning that it creates a greater sense of partnership with the birds. Hand feeding treats in the loft like peanuts or seeds also builds the relationship and trust between the fancier and his birds.)

Working with Older Birds

Birds with racing experience are smart. They know what they're doing and only need an ongoing level of physical conditioning to remain at a high performance level. The only time you would have to start over with training tosses would be an instance when an adult bird is relocated to a new loft. Under those methods, the routine of progressively lengthier tosses is exactly the same.

Deciding when to fly a bird depends on the bird. Some pigeons, for instance, deliver faster race times when they have young in the nest. The most important thing for any fancier is to know the individual bird and to cater to its strengths. "Old pigeon" racing, that done by birds of more than 1 year of age offers some of the most exciting results.

Pigeons get better at what they do over time because their homing incentives are stronger.

The Fine Points of Training

There are many fine points to working with racing pigeons that come from experience and hours of conversation with experienced pigeon fanciers. My purpose here has been to illustrate that at the most basic level pigeon racing is not a difficult sport – at least for the keepers. The birds do all the really hard work and take all the serious risks.

There are many systems for motivating pigeons to return to their home loft, endless theories about when to pair birds, which birds should race, which should be kept at home, and on and on and on. The fine points of racing pigeons can be discussed literally for a lifetime as you have your own successes and failures and develop the methods that will work for you and your birds.

There really is no one "right" way. So long as your birds are happy and are winning, you're doing it "right."

Afterword

In the foreword of this text, I asked readers to simply cultivate an appreciation for the remarkable and long-standing relationship between pigeons and man. Now, at the end of the book, I hope that goal has been met and perhaps surpassed.

If you are now deciding how to connect with experienced pigeon fanciers to learn, first hand, about loft design and husbandry, welcome to what will be both a passion and a pleasure.

Pigeon keeping is a "scalable" pastime. You can maintain a small loft with just a few birds primarily for the pleasure of keeping these lovely creatures as pets. You may race a few birds, or opt to breed pigeons for sale to others. Perhaps the fancy breeds have caught your eye and your plan is to raise show birds.

This is, ostensibly, a book about pigeon racing. The sport is somewhat specialized and often misunderstood. In that regard, my intent has been to offer straightforward and simple introductory explanations of how pigeons are trained and raced.

I am, however, a great appreciator of these birds in all their forms. Many times I attend pigeon shows for the sheer enjoyment of the diversity of species.

I especially like to attend shows where young people are exhibiting pigeons and in the process learning valuable lessons about the kind treatment of the remarkable creatures with whom we share this planet.

A pigeon's homing prowess is nothing short of a navigational miracle, but that's not all that is amazing about these birds. They are loyal. They learn well. They enjoy what they do. They are, truly, avian endurance athletes.

Regardless of the level on which you engage the pigeon passion, I know it will bring you hours of enjoyment. You will learn as much for your birds as they will learn from you. Good luck and good flying!

Appendix I - List of Pigeon Breeds

A

Aachen Lacquer Shield Owl
Aachen Pouter
Aargau Peak Crested
Absy Egyptian Swift
African Owl
Agaran Boinije
Ahmar Gohzar Egyptian Swift
Alpine Swift
Altenburger Trumpeter
American Bohemian Pouter
American Flying Baldhead
American Flying Flight
American Flying Tumbler
American Giant Homer
American Giant Rumbler
American Giant Runt
American Modern Flight
American Roller
American Show Racer
American Strasser
Anbary Asmar Egyptian Swift
Ancient Tumbler
Antwerp
Antwerp Smerle
Arabian Trumpeter
Arad Barred Highflier
Archangel
Archangel White Trjasuni

Armenian Tumbler
Armenian Highflier
Asiatic Crack Tumbler
Australian Performing Tumbler
Australian Saddleback Tumbler

B

Baku Boinije
Baska Tumbler
Barb
Bavarian Pouter
Beak-Crested Jacobin
Belgian Ringbeater
Berlin Medium Face Tumbler
Berlin Long Face Tumbler
Berlin Short Faced Tumbler
Bernburg
Berne Half Beak
Berne Peak Crested
Bernhardin Magpie
Birmingham Roller
Blondinette
Blue Tumbler of Cluj
Bohemian Pouter
Bohmentaub
Bokhara Trumpeter
Bokhara Tumbler
Bolk Egyptian Swift
Boston Blue Tumbler
Bremen Tumbler
Breslauer Tumbler

British Show Racer
Brunner Pouter
Bucharest Ciung Highflier
Bucharest Show Tumbler
Buda Grizzle Budapest Short Face Tumbler
Budapest Highflier
Budapest Muffed Tumbler
Budapest Muffled Stork
Budapest Short Face Tumbler
Bursa

C

Carneau
Cassel Tumbler
Catalonian Head and Neck Tumbler
Catalonian Laced Bordench Mondain
Catalonian Tumbler
Cauchois
Central Asiatic Roller
Chinese Nasal Tufted
Chinese Owl
Clean Legged Fullhead Swallow
Clean Legged Spot Swallow
Coburg Lark
Colillano Pouter
Cologne Tumbler
Crescent
Crested Soultz
Cumulet
Czech Bagdad
Czech Ice Pouter

Czech Muffed Tumbler
Czech Trumpeter

D

Damascene
Danish Suabian
Danish Tumbler
Danzig Highflyer
Dewlap
Domestic Show Flight
Donek
Double Crested Priest
Dragoon
Dresden Trumpeter
Duchess
Dutch Highflier

E

Ebling Whitehead
Egyptian Swift
Egyptian Tumbler
Eichbuhl
Elster Pouter
Elster Purzler
English Barb
English Carrier
English Exhibition Homer
English Fantail
English Long Face Tumbler
English Longface Muff Tumbler

English Magpie
English Owl
English Pouter
English Short Faced Tumbler
English Show Homer
English Trumpeter
Erlau Tumbler
Escompadissa Tumbler
Exhibition Flying Tippler

F

Fantail
Fat Shan Blue
Felegyhazer Tumbler
Fish Eye Roller
Florentine
Flying Oriental Roller
Flying Performing Roller
Flying Saddle Homer
Flying Tippler
Fork-Tailed
Franconian Heart Magpie
Franconian Toy Self
Franconian Trumpeter
Franconian Velvet Shield
French Bagdad
French Mondain
French Pouter
Frillback

G

Gaditano Pouter
Galaţi roller
Genuine Homer
German Beauty Homer
German Beak-Crested
German Colored Tail Owl
German Double-Crested
German Long Face Tumbler
German Modena
German Nun
German Shield Owl
Ghent Cropper
Giant American Crest
Giant Mallorquina Runt
Giant Runt
Gier
Gorguero Pouter
Granadino Pouter
Groninger Slenke
Gumbinnen White Head Tumbler

H

Hague Highflier
Halaby Egyptian Swift
Hamburg Sticken
Hamburg Tumbler
Hana Pouter
Hanover Tumbler
Helmet
Hessian Pouter
Hindi Fantail

Hollander
Holle Cropper
Hungarian
Hungarian Buga Pigeon
Hungarian Egri Tumbler
Hungarian Giant House Pigeon
Hungarian Giant Pouter
Hungarian Highflier
Hungarian Short Beaker
Huppé Picard
Hyacinth

I

Ice Pigeon
Indian Fantail
Indian Fantasy
Indian Gola
Indian Mondain
Indian Pearl Highflier
Indian Pigeon
Iranian Highflier
Iran Roller
Italian Owl

J

Jacobin
Jerezano Pouter
Jewel Mondain
Jiennense Pouter
K

Kaluga Turmani
Karakand Fantail
Karakandy Egyptian Swift
Kazan Tumbler
Kelebek
Kiev Tumbler
King
Kiskunfelegyhaza Tumbler
Kojook Egyptian Swift
Komorner Tumbler
Konigsberg Moorhead
Koros Tumbler

L

Lacene
Lahore
Laudino Sevillano Pouter
Lebanon
Lenardo
Lille Pouter
Lotan
Lucerne Gold Collar

M

Macedonian Turbit
Magpie
Majorcan Bort Runt
Majorcan Esbart Roller
Maltese
Marchenero Pouter

Mariola
Markische Magpie Tumbler
Martham
Memel Highflier
Mesawed Egyptian Swift
Micholaiyvski Shield Tumbler
Miniature American Crested
Modena
Modern Show Flight
Modern Spanish Thief Pouter
Mookee
Montauben
Moravian White Head
Morrillero Alicantino Pouter
Moroncelo Pouter
Moscat
Moscovite Tumbler
Moulter
Muffed helmet
Munsterland Field Pigeon

N

Norwegian Tumbler
Norwich Cropper
Novi Sad Short Face Tumbler
Nun
Nuremberg Lark
Nurnberg Swallow
Nis's White-Tail Highflyer

O

Old Dutch Capuchine
Old Dutch Tumbler
Old Dutch Turbit
Old Fashioned Oriental Frill
Old German Cropper
Old German Moorhead
Old German Nun
Old German Owl
Old German Turbit
Old Holland Pouter
Old Style English Flying Saddle Tumbler
Oriental Frill
Oriental Roller
Oriental Turbit
Ostrava Bagdad
Otati Egyptian Swift

P

Pakistani Highflier
Pappatacci
Parlor Roller
Parlor Tumbler
Persian Highflyer
Pheasant Pigeon
Piacention
Pigmy Mariola
Pigmy Pouter
Polish Barb
Polish Gansel Tumbler

Polish Helmet
Polish Highflier
Polish Kronen Tumbler
Polish Lynx
Polish Orlik
Polish Owll
Pomeranian Pouter
Pomeranian Show Crest
Portuguese Breeder
Portuguese Tumbler
Posen Colored Head Tumbler
Poster
Prachen Kanik
Prager Short Face Tumbler
Prague Medium Face Tumbler
Ptarmigan

Q

Quiet Roller

R

Racing Homer
Rafeno Pouter
Rakovnik Roller
Rawson Short Face Tumbler
Regensburg Tumbler
Rehani Egyptian Swift
Reinaugen Tumbler
Reversewing Color Pigeon
Reversewing Pouter

Rhine Ringbeater
Roller Pigeon
Romagnol
Romanian Argintiu Tumbler
Romanian Beard
Romanian Black-Cherry Tumbler
Romanian Blind Tumbler
Romanian Blue Barred Whitetail
Romanian Coffee-Colored Tumbler
Romanian Gagiu
Romanian Moriscar Roller
Romanian Naked-Neck Tumbler
Romanian Silvery Tumbler
Romanian Orbetean Tumbler
Romanian Tshoong Tumbler
Romanian Whitetail Tumbler
Romanian Satu-Mare Tumbler
Roshan Chirag
Royal Snow Tumbler
Russian Akkermann Tumbler
Russian Martini
Russian Tumbler
Rzhev Startail Tumbler

S

Saar Pigeon
Safi Egyptian Swift
Saint
Satinette
Satu-Mare Tumbler
Saxon Breast Pigeon

Saxon Fairy Swallow
Saxon Field Pigeon
Saxon Monk
Saxon Pouter
Saxon Priest
Saxon Shield
Saxon Spot
Saxon Stork
Saxon White Tail
Scandaroon
Schalaster Pouter
Schmalkender Moorhead
Schmolin
Schoneberger Streifige Tumbler
Seraphim Pigeon
Serbian Highflier
Shack Kee
Shakhsharli
Show Cumulet
Show Racing Homer
Show Tippler
Silesian Moorhead
Silesian Pouter
Silesian White Head
Silky Fantail
Single Crested Priest
Slovak Pouter
Sottobanca
South German Charcoal Lark
South German Latz
South German Monk
South German Moorhead

South German Shield
South German Spot
South German Tigermohr
South German White Tail
Spaniard
Spanish Bagdad
Spanish Barb
Spanish Flamenca Runt
Spanish Frillback Bagadette
Spanish Gabacho Runt
Spanish Little Friar Tumbler
Spanish Mondain
Spanish Monjin
Spanish Naked Neck Pigeon
Spanish Nun
Spanish Owl
Spanish Owl Pouter
Spanish Thief Pouter
Spangeled Magpie Purzler of Satu-Mare
Srebrniak
Starling
Stargard Shaker
Starwitzer Pouter
Steinheim Bagdad
Stellerkrofer
Stettiner Tumbler
Steiger Pouter
Stork Pigeon
Stralsunder Highflier
Strasser
Sverdlovsk Blue-Gray Mottle-Headed
Swallow

Swing Pouter
Swiss Crescent
Swiss Mondain
Syrian Bagdad
Syrian Coop Tumbler
Syrian Fantail
Syrian Halabi
Syrian Sabuni Tumbler
Syrian Swift
Syrian Turbiteen
Szegediner Highflier

T

Taganrog Tumbler
Taqlaji
Texan Pioneer
Thai Fantail
Thai Laugher
Thurgau Peak Crested
Thuringian Breast Pigeon
Thuringen Field Pigeon
Thuringian Goldkafertaube
Thuringian Pouter
Thuringian Self Colored
Thuringian Shield
Thuringian Spot
Thuringian Stork
Thuringian Swallow
Thuringian White Bib
Thuringian White Head
Thuringian Wingpigeon

Tiger Swallow
Tippler
Timisora Tumbler
Transylvanian Double-Crested Tumbler
Tumbler of Arad
Tumbler of Botoşani
Tumbler of Craiova
Tumbler of Kiev
Tumbler of Transylvania
Tumbler of Yassy
Tung Koon Paak
Turbit
Turbiteen Mövchen
Turisian Owl
Turkish Pigeon

U

Ural Striped Maned

V

Valencian Figurita
Valencian Giant Tenant
Valencian Homer
Valencian Magany Homer
Valencian Peter Runt
Valencian Pouter
Verkehrtflügelfarbentaube
Vienna
Vienna Gansel
Vienna Highflier

Vienna Medium Face Tumbler
Vienna Muffed Tumbler
Vienna Short Face Tumbler
Vienna White Shield Tumbler
Vogtland
Volga Russian Tumbler
Voorburg Shield Cropper

W

Warsaw Schmetterling
West of England Tumbler
Wuürttemberg Moorhead

Z

Zitterhall
Zurich White Tail

Relevant Websites

American Racing Pigeon Union
www.pigeon.org

Arizona Pigeon Club
www.azpigeonclub.org

Basic Pigeon Needs
mumtazticloft.com/PigeonBasicNeeds.asp

Beginners Guide to Racing Pigeons
www.pigeonmad.com/beginners_guide_to_racing_pigeons.
php

The Pigeon in History
www.pigeoncontrolresourcecentre.org/html/the-pigeon-in-
history.html

Instructions on Reception, Care and Training of Homing
Pigeons
www.history.navy.mil/library/special/homing_pigeons.htm

International Federation of American Homing Pigeon
www.ifpigeon.com

International Poultry Breeders Association
www.featheredfamilies.com

National Pigeon Association
www.npausa.com

New England Pigeon Supply
www.nepigeonsupplies.com

Pigeons and Doves - Feeding
www.vcahospitals.com/main/pet-health-
information/article/animal-health/pigeons-and-doves-
feeding/918

Pigeon Paradise
www.pipa.be

Pigeon Racing: The Basics
www.pigeonbasics.com/articles/article94.html

Royal Pigeon Racing Association
www.rpra.org/

Pigeon Wiki
pigeons.wikia.com

Racing Pigeon – An Independent Weekly Publication
racingpigeon.co.uk

Racing Pigeon Digest – Magazine
www.racingpigeondigest.com

Racing Pigeon Mall
www.racingpigeonmall.com

Things to Consider When Breeding Your Pigeons
mannyguerrero.jimdo.com/pigeon-articles/things-to-
consider-when-breeding-your-pigeons/

Training Racing Pigeons
www.speedpigeon.com/training_racing_pigeons.htm

Glossary

A

ace hole - The favorite trap door you want your birds to use on race day.

airline - The airline is the straight line from the loft to the release point in the race. The distance is computed in the nearest 1/1000 of a mile, with the computation approved by a civil engineering firm or confirmed by GPS.

air sacs - A system of nine interconnected sacs extend through a pigeon's body to circulate air.

arm - A pigeon's humerus, or arm, is the bone in the wing projecting directly away from the body.

arrival time – The official time that a pigeon clocks in at the loft in a race.

Ash - An Ash is a light tan Racing Homer without wing bars. Sometimes these birds are called a Barless Mealy.

AU - The acronym for the American Racing Pigeon Union, Inc., which is the largest such organization in the United States.

average speed - Average speed is the best performance in a loft calculated by adding the sum of all the birds clocked in to the loft divided by the number of races flown. If a loft misses a race it is no longer eligible to compete for any average speed award given for the season.

aviary - An aviary is a wire enclosure that is attached to the loft to allow pigeons to sun themselves. The aviary is also used to allow young birds to familiarize themselves with the surroundings outside the loft before they are allowed outside. Coming in and out of the aviary also gets young birds accustomed to the idea of the trap door.

B

balanced - "Balanced" is a term that refers to how a pigeon feels in your hand. Good balance is essential in racing pigeons, but identifying it is something that comes with experience.

bananas - "Bananas" is the term used to describe the pattern in the scales on a pigeon's legs and feet.

band - A metal or plastic band is attached to a pigeon's leg containing information like bird number, birth year, club or organization, and contact information for the owner.

banding - Banding occurs when racing pigeon's are 7 days old. This is when the bird's unique identification information is attached. Banding also occurs when birds are prepared to be released for a race and their temporary race number is affixed to the other leg.

bars - Bars are bands of color on the back part of the top surface of a pigeon's wing.

bastard flight - The bastard flight is a small, flight-like feather located at the joint of the wing butt.

beak angle - The beak angle is formed between the beak and forehead.

beard - Pigeons that have feathers and excess flesh directly under the lower beak are described as having a "beard."

bib - The bib is the color pattern on the front part of a pigeon's neck.

billing - Billing is the action of a female pigeon reaching down a male's throat to receive an offering of regurgitated food. Often likened to kissing, the behavior is a precursor to mating.

blocky - A body that is short, and broad is called "blocky." Alternate terms include "apple bodied" or "cobby."

bloom - "Bloom" is a powdery white dust found in a pigeon's feathers.

Blue Bar - A Blue Bar is a light blue to grayish Racing Homer marked with two black bars on the back part of the wing's top surface. Often referred to simply as a "Blue."

Blue Check - A Blue Check is a light blue to grayish Racing Homer marked with a black-checked pattern on the wing's top surface.

bobs - The bobs are lightweight aluminum rods a pigeon pushes against to go through the trap and into the loft. Normally the arrangement is for a one way entrance.

bowing - Bowing is one of the courtship behaviors exhibited by a male pigeon, which includes puffing out the neck feathers, lowering the head, and turning in circles.

breaking point - The breaking point is that theoretical point at which an individual bird must break away from a flock to win the race. After being liberated, the returning pigeons mainly fly together until they begin to break off and go to their own lofts.

breast - The breast is the region of the body containing the pectoral muscles as well as the bird's crop.

bull eye - A bull eye is one that is very dark in color with a thick iris that displays black or dark "breeding grooves."

C

candy - Candy is a mixture of small grains used to entice the birds to trap faster.

canker – Canker is a disease of the mouth and throat that also affects respiration in pigeons.

carrying crate - The carrying crate is a box typically made of wood and canvas. There is a top door, and a canvas flap release door on the side. The crate is used to transport and then release racing pigeons.

cere - The cere is the bare skin found around a pigeon's eye.

Champion Bird - A Champion Bird is the pigeon that flew best and placed highest the greatest amount of times in a series of races.

Champion Loft - A Champion Loft is the loft that accumulates the greatest number of high points for winning birds in a series of races.

Checker - A Checker is a Racing Homer marked with a colored checked pattern on the top surface of its wings.

circling - Circling is the act of a pigeon flying in a circular pattern over the loft either for exercise or returning from a training toss or race.

clock - A clock is the timing device used to record the arrival time of pigeons in a race.

clock opening – The clock opening is the event where participants gather to calculate the speed of the birds in the race and determine the winner. This applies primarily to races in which traditional timing devices are used.

clutch - A "clutch" is the complete set of eggs laid by a female pigeon.

cock – A cock is a male pigeon

common - A "common" is any pigeon not a thoroughbred racing bird that shows up in the yard. The presence of such birds is not desirable.

condition - "Condition" refers to a pigeon's general health including the perfection of the feathers and muscle tone.

contagious – A contagious disease is one that can be transmitted from one pigeon to another.

conveyor - A conveyor is the person who transports racing pigeons to the release point for the race.

cooing - "Cooing" is the sound that pigeons make during their courtship.

coop – "Coop" is an alternate term for the facility or enclosure in which pigeons are kept. Typically the term "loft" is preferred.

corkiness - "Corkiness" describes a pigeon that has a light weight and is in good race condition.

countermark - The countermark is the rubber or stretchable numbered band placed on a racing's pigeon's leg before a race and is the means by which the bird is both verified as an official entry and timed at its return to the loft.

cover feathers - The cover feathers, which attach to the upper wing, comprise the greatest part of the wing surface.

coverts - The coverts are the small feathers of a pigeon's wings and tail.

crate – the crate is a container in which pigeons are placed for shipping to the race release point.

crest – A crest is formed by feathers that are reversed in direction on the top of a pigeon's head.

crooked keel - A crooked keel is a deformed breast bone, which is considered a flaw in a pigeon.

crop - The crop is a bird's first stomach. Feed is stored in this fleshy pocket in the neck for up to 12 hours before passing on to the stomach and intestines.

cross breeding - Cross breeding refers to mating birds that have no relationship within the previous five generations or unrelated birds for the purpose of avoiding hazardous in-breeding.

cull - A cull is an unwanted bird, or the process by which such birds are eliminated.

D

dam - A dam is the female member of a mated pair of pigeons.

day bird - A day bird is one that is released on the day of a race that returns home before dark on the same day.

dovecote - Dovecote is another term for a pigeon loft or coop.

down - Down is the fuzzy yellow body covering on a newly hatched pigeon.

drag - The term "drag" refers to the location of the majority of lofts in a race.

driving - Driving is the behavior of a male pigeon when he runs behind his hen at close range pecking and chasing her into the nest box. It is a guarding action.

drop - Pigeons returning from a race arrive in groups referred to as "drops."

dropper - A dropper is a fancy pigeon released in the yard. The bird flies straight to the landing board, which coaxes the racing pigeons to land and come into the loft.

droppings – Dropping are pigeon excrement.

E

egg-bound - When a pigeon hen cannot lay a fully formed egg, she is said to be egg-bound.

entry sheet - The entry sheet is the form that lists the birds entered in a race and provides their identification data.

eye sign – "Eye sign" is a theory that suggests characteristics of a pigeon's eye indicate the bird's ability to win races or breed successfully.

F

fancier – A fancier is a person who breeds pigeons or keeps them for competitive or show purposes.

fancy pigeon - Fancy pigeons are breeds kept for show rather than racing. These birds often have unique shapes, feather arrangements, body conformation, or color / pattern.

feather merchant - A feather merchant is an individual who sells birds. Such people are typically the top flyers in the racing world with outstanding records for raising champion birds.

"first bird in" - The term "first bird in" refers to the first pigeon to return to the loft from a training toss or race.

flagging - Flagging is the practice of forcing the birds to fly around the loft for a set period of time to get physical exercise.

flight – Flight refers to the 20 large feathers of a pigeon's wing. The 10 outer feathers are the primaries.

flyers - Flyers are the pigeon fanciers racing their birds in any given season.

form - "Form" is a term to describe the condition of a racing pigeon.

fret marks - Fret marks are horizontal marks or deformities on the feathers caused by stress or poor nutrition.

frill - A frill is a line of reversed feathers on the neck or crop.

G

girth - Girth refers to the circumference of the pigeon's body.

grit – Grit refers to calcium and other particles, often supplied via crushed oyster shells, fed to pigeons to help them digest the grain in their diet.

grizzle - Grizzle is a pattern comprised of two colors on individual feathers, for instance white flecked with gray.

H

hawk bait - Pigeons with a lot of white on their bodies are often characterized as "hawk bait" because they are easily targeted by birds of prey.

hen - A hen is a female pigeon.

hold over - A hold over occurs when pigeons cannot be released for some reason (generally inclement weather) and the start of the race is delayed.

homer – Shorthand reference for homing pigeons.

hoople - A hoople is a device similar in appearance to a tennis racket, but with a longer handle. It is used to herd pigeons into the trap.

I

in-breeding – In-breeding is the practice of mating closely related pigeons to retain desirable genetic qualities in the offspring.

J

jewing - The jewing is the portion of the wattle located on the lower beak.

K

keel - The keel is the bone running down the middle of the breast. It is the point of attachment for the pectoral muscles.

keratin - Keratin is the protein that forms feathers.

kick - "Kick" refers to the action of turning the knob on a traditional race timer to stamp the exact time.

kicking - "Kicking" is the action of setting multiple race clocks to the same time.

kit - A kit is a flock of pigeons flying together as a team.

L

landing board - The landing board is a large flat surface on which the birds alight before entering the trap and going into the loft.

late hatch - Late hatches are the third and fourth round of birds born in a year that are too young to enter races.

liberation - Liberation is the act of letting pigeons loose from their shipping crates.

liberator - A liberator is the person who turns pigeons loose at the start of a race.

loft – A loft is a structure designed for the purpose of housing and nurturing pigeons.

loft flying – Loft flying refers to the release of pigeons inside a loft to exercise.

loft break - Loft breaking is the process of teaching young birds where they live and creating in them a desire to return to their loft when they are released.

M

mandible - The mandible is the beak or bill of a bird.

Mealy - A mealy is a light tan Racing Homer marked with red-brown bars across the back part of the wings' top surface molt – Molting is the natural process of shedding feathers, which occurs in the late summer and early fall.

N

natural system - The natural system is one in which racing birds are kept in pairs, sitting on eggs, or rearing their young as race motivators.

nicking - Nicking refers to a family of racing pigeons that cross well and produce winners across multiple generations.

night flight - "Night flight" refers to birds that refuse to land after their normal evening exercise period and fly all night.

O

old bird – An old bird is a racing pigeon that is more than one year of age.

on the drop - "On the drop" refers to the number of birds that came in and landed first.

one loft race - One loft racing is an event in which all the birds are housed and trained in a single loft and race to that loft from a designated release point.

out-cross - Out-crossing is the practice of mating unrelated families of racing pigeons.

overfly - When one loft is located farther from the release point than another, the far loft is said to "overfly" the near one.

P

pectorals - The pectorals are the large muscles lying on both sides of the keel.

pedigree - A pedigree is the written ancestry and racing record of an individual racing pigeon.

perch - The perch is an elevated place on which each pigeon sits and to which the individual birds become strongly attached.

Pied - A Pied pigeon is a Racing Homer with white feathers on its neck or head.

pin feather - A pin feather is a growing feather on young birds that has not yet broken through the shaft.

pipping - Pipping is the process by which young birds chip their way out of the egg shell during hatching.

plumage - Plumage is a bird's general feathering.

poles - Poles are sticks of bamboo or wood used to herd birds to the trap.

pot eggs - Pot eggs are wooden or plastic eggs used to replace real eggs when hatching is undesirable. They are typically used with old birds during racing season so the birds won't become exhausted tending to offspring.

primaries - The primaries are the last ten large flight feathers on a pigeon's wing.

prisoner - A prisoner is a pigeon that is never allowed out of the loft. Typically refers to a bird acquired from someone else that is too old to loft break.

pumpers - Pumpers are pigeons that are used as foster parents.

pumping - Pumping is the process of taking eggs from the best breeding pigeons in the loft and putting them under foster parents or "pumpers" to be hatched.

R

race - A race is competitive event designed to determine the fastest performing birds.

race course - The race course is the direction in which the races will be run for the coming season. Direction remains constant over a season.

race season - Typically there are two racing seasons per year, one for young birds and one for old birds.

race secretary - The individual chosen to determine if conditions are favorable for the release of birds to begin a race.

race station - The race station is the designated point of release for the birds in a race.

race team - The race team are all the pigeons used during a season.

Racing Homer - A Racing Homer is a pigeon whose ability to return home quickly and accurately has been selectively bred over hundreds of generations.

Red Check - A Red Check is a light red Racing Homer with a dark red to brown checked pattern on the top surface of its wing.

road training – Road training is the act of crating birds, carrying them to a distance, and releasing them to fly home. Also called tossing

running board - A running board is a horizontal 4 x 6 inch / 10.16 – 15.24 cm wide board in the aviary on which the pigeons can stand.

S

secondaries - The secondaries are the ten smaller flight feathers on the pigeon's wing lying next to the body.

settling - Settling is the act of acclimating young birds to the loft and/or letting the birds outside for the first time.

settling cage - A settling cage is a wire cage placed on the landing board that covers the front of the trap. It is part of the process of loft breaking.

silky - "Silky" is a term that describes healthy feathers.

single toss – Single tossing is the process of road training only one pigeon.

sire - The sire is the male in a mated pair of pigeons.

smash – A "smash" occurs when no birds return from a training toss or race. This may be due to bad weather or poor training.

squab – A squab is a baby pigeon.

squeaker – A squeaker is a pigeon aged 2-8 weeks.

stall trap - A stall trap is designed with multiple partitions so that only one pigeon may enter at a time. A locking device keeps the pigeons in the stall until the race band is removed. The bird cannot enter the loft until the fancier unlocks the trap.

stockings - Stockings are feathers on the legs or feet.

T

team - A team is the group of pigeons being raced or flown.

throw back – A throw back is a color pattern that does not resemble either of the parents but is similar to a distant relative.

toss – A toss is the process of bringing pigeons to an area and releasing them to fly back to the loft. Also called road training.

trap – A trap is a device that allows a pigeon to enter the loft, but prevents the bird from exiting.

trapping – Trapping is the official time when a bird enters that loft.

treading - Treading is the sexual act of the cock jumping on to the hen's back.

tripping - Tripping is the process of exercising racing pigeons in the immediate vicinity of their loft, flying for long periods of time. Also called ranging or routing.

U

Unikon - Unikon is an electronic clocking system. Antennas in the trap read chip rings on the pigeon's leg to record the exact second the bird enters the trap.

V

variation time – The variation time is the difference between a fancier's clock and that of the club, which can be avoided with proper synchronization.

velocity – Velocity is the average speed attained by a pigeon during a race measured in meters or yards per minute.

vent bones - The vent bones are two small bones located directly behind and on either side of the breast bone and under the tail.

W

wattle - The wattle is the fleshy covering of the nostrils behind the upper beak.

weaning – Weaning is the process of separating a young pigeon from its parents to fend for itself, usually accomplished around 28 days of age.

White Flight - A White Flight is a Racing Homer with one or more white primary-flights (the large wing feathers).

widowhood - Widowhood is a racing system in which a male is only allowed to see his mate after coming home from a race. It is a method of motivating the fastest flight response possible. (There are many versions of widowhood used by fanciers.)

Y

young bird - A young bird is a pigeon that is not a year old.

YPM - YPM is the abbreviation for yards-per-minute. It is the measurement used to give the speed of the pigeon when the bird has been officially clocked coming off a race.

Index

www.LollyBrown.com - **Find more books available by this author.**

www.NRBpublishing.com - **Find more books available by this publisher.**

Feeding Baby
Cynthia Cherry
978-1941070000

Axolotl
Lolly Brown
978-0989658430

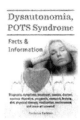

Dysautonomia POTS
Syndrome
Frederick Earlstein
978-0989658485

Degenerative Disc
Disease Explained
Frederick Earlstein
978-0989658485

Sinusitis, Hay Fever,
Allergic Rhinitis Explained
Frederick Earlstein
978-1941070024

Wicca
Riley Star
978-1941070130

Zombie Apocalypse
Rex Cutty
978-1941070154

Capybara
Lolly Brown
978-1941070062

Eels As Pets
Lolly Brown
978-1941070167

Scabies and Lice Explained
Frederick Earlstein
978-1941070017

Saltwater Fish As Pets
Lolly Brown
978-0989658461

Torticollis Explained
Frederick Earlstein
978-1941070055

Kennel Cough
Lolly Brown
978-0989658409

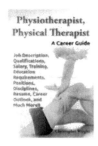

Physiotherapist, Physical
Therapist
Christopher Wright
978-0989658492

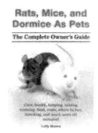

Rats, Mice, and Dormice
As Pets
Lolly Brown
978-1941070079

Wallaby and Wallaroo Care
Lolly Brown
978-1941070031

CPSIA information can be obtained at www.ICGtesting.com
Printed in the USA
LVOW10s0227300115

424990LV00032B/675/P